Haiku

one breath poetry

Written
and
Illustrated
by

Naomi Wakan

HEIAN

Haiku : one breath poetry

ISBN : 0-89346-846-0

Illustrated by Naomi Wakan
Design and layout by Elias Wakan

Heian International, Inc.
Publishers
1815 West 205th Street, Suite # 301
Torrance, CA 90501

Printed in the U.S.A.

Dedicated to the memory of the late Leon Zolbrod

Acknowledgments

My thanks to Japan Air Lines for permission to use the haiku from *Out of the Mouths* and to the JAL Foundation for those in *Haiku by the Children*. Thanks also to Princeton University Press for permission to quote from Daisetz T. Suzuki's *Zen and Japanese Culture* and to Asian Humanities Press for permission to quote one of David Lanoue's translations from *Issa: Cup-of-Tea Poems*. The haiku from the JAL student competition were translated in each country. All others are in my own words unless otherwise indicated.

I am indebted to Cathrine Conings, Satoko Hashigasako, Perry Millar and Carolyn Bateman for their advice, and am especially grateful to the students and teachers of Windsor House in North Vancouver and Henry Hudson Elementary School in Vancouver for letting me try out some ideas with them. Most of all, I am thankful to my husband, Elias, for his helpful criticism and patience. All opinions and errors remain my own.

Table of Contents

Preface

This book is about the world's shortest form of poetry. Sometimes called "one-breath" poetry, since their 17 syllables can be recited between an in-breath and an out-breath, haiku's briefness appeals to everyone.

In haiku, pronounced *hī kōō*, every word counts. Robert Blyth, who wrote four famous books on haiku, said that a haiku was like a finger pointing to the moon and that if the finger is covered in jewels (unnecessary words), we would only look at the finger and forget about looking at the moon. Because each word must count, it is difficult to write a really good haiku; on the other hand, because haiku are short, they are simple to try.

The best thing about "one-breath" poems is that anyone can write them; whether rich or poor, clever or not so clever, male or female, young or old (even Japanese or non-Japanese), everyone can write haiku. Writing haiku is not some secret thing that only a few chosen people can do, although to write a good one, one that makes the reader sigh "Ah . . . " with satisfaction, well, that may take several years of trying.

Haiku:

Introducing Haiku

◾

Haiku, the most popular form of Japanese poetry, has won the hearts of people around the world. And where better to begin a book about haiku than with the most famous one. It was written by Japan's best-known haiku poet – Bashō, who is generally considered to be the father of haiku poetry.

An old pond . . .
a frog leaps in,
the sound of water.

Furuike ya	/ *kawazu tobikomu*	/ *mizu no oto*
old pond . . .	/ frog jump in	/ water's sound

Even though Japanese haiku were often written in one line, rather than in three, haiku poets were always aware that the poem was in three parts – the first part having five syllables, the second seven syllables and the third five.

5 syllables	7 syllables	5 syllables
Fu-ru-i-ke-ya	ka-wa-zu-to-bi-ko-mu	mi-zu-no-o-to

In this book, the Japanese will be given if possible so that the 5-7-5 pattern can be seen, though you will notice that some Japanese haiku have slightly more or fewer syllables than the typical 5-7-5 form. In addition, you may have already noticed (and it will be explained later) that the Japanese syllable unit (*onji*) differs somewhat from English.

one breath poetry

Here is a popular haiku by the poet Issa (another one of Japan's four great haiku poets: Bashō, Buson, Issa and Shiki).

Skinny frog
Don't give up,
Issa is rooting for you.

Yasegaeru	/ *makeruna Issa*	/ *koko-ni ari*
skinny frog	/ don't be beaten Issa	/ here is

5 syllables	7 syllables	5 syllables
ya-se-ga-e-ru	ma-ke-ru-na-I-s-sa	ko-ko-ni-a-ri

By the way, in Japanese, the same word can be both singular and plural, so that "haiku" can mean either one poem or more than one poem. In case you might be thinking that young people cannot produce such great haiku as the ones by Bashō and Issa, here is a lovely image by 12-year-old Lou Jia from China.

Spring thunder –
surprised, the little turtle
waves its neck around.

And here is a fine haiku by Shinya Ida of Japan, written when he was in Grade 1!

In our iris-blossom-bath
grandpa and little sister
are singing songs.

This is a wonderful picture of generations. It was written for what used to be called Boy's Day (now called Children's Day), a celebration during which iris leaves were put in the family bath to frighten away illness and evil spirits.

Some Japanese think it is impossible for non-Japanese to understand haiku. Luckily for us, however, many Japanese people delight in haiku written by non-Japanese and are happy that the spirit behind haiku is linking so many different cultures around the world.

Beginning to Write Haiku

Look out the window, then write a few sentences about what you see. Don't write about what you feel or what you think, just write what you see. Perhaps you will write something like this:

> "The back alley, which is usually dirty and filled with garbage bags, is now covered in a pile of very white snow. A black cat is sitting on a fence looking at the snow."

Now that you have written your scene, go back and take out all the words that don't add to the picture, all those "jewels on the finger" that prevent us from looking at the moon.

> "The back alley ~~(which is)~~ usually dirty ~~(and filled with garbage bags,)~~ is now covered in ~~(a pile of very white)~~ snow. A black cat ~~(is sitting on a fence)~~ look~~(ing)~~s at the snow."

Can you make your description even tighter, taking out as many "jeweled" words as possible? Get your description down to about 10 words.

Haiku:

The back alley
  covered in snow . . .
    a black cat smiles.

Did you manage to write a small scene like this? If so, you are getting close to being able to write haiku. As we continue through the book, your idea of what a haiku is will get clearer and clearer, and your haiku will please you more and more.

What? Where? and When?

Haiku is simply what is happening in this place, at this moment. As Kenneth Yasuda (a haiku authority) states, the haiku tells you **what** has made you stop and write a haiku, **where** you stopped and **when** you stopped.

Look at the following haiku by Issa and see if you can find the what, when and where in each of them.

In the cherry blossoms' shade, there are no complete strangers.

Hana no kage   / *aka no*   *tanin*   *wa*   / *nakari*   *keri*
blossoms' shade / complete strangers   / must not . . .

The what is "nobody is a complete stranger," the where is "under the blossoming cherry trees," the when is "when the first blossoms come out" (everyone in Japan would know that the mention of blossoms means cherry-blossom time). Issa is telling us that when everyone is admiring the new blossoms, people feel warmth towards one another and talk freely as they would not normally do with strangers in daily life. What a lot of information in 10 words!

Keri is a word used in haiku when the poet would like you to pause and think about the words he or she has written. I will be telling you more about such words soon.

Haiku:

*Radish farmer
pointing the way
with a radish.*

| *Daikon-hiki* | / | *daikon de* | *michi wo* | / *oshie keri* |
| radish puller | / | radish with | road | / showing . . . |

Here the what is the radish, the when is harvest time and the where is at the edge of the farmer's field. This is quite a funny image as the farmer is so engrossed in picking radishes that he doesn't realize he is using a radish, instead of his finger, to point the way to a passing stranger. Maybe Issa is telling us that it is good to be so absorbed in the task we have in hand.

Here is a good answer to what, when and where in a haiku by Nahanni Stevenson from British Columbia, Canada, who wrote it when in Grade 6.

*A heron rises
In the middle of the swamp
Under the full moon.*

Sometimes, instead of answers to the three questions what, when, and where, haiku poets try to name one object that is everlasting, one that is passing, and something that links the two. In the above haiku, the moon could be the everlasting element, the heron the passing one, with the swamp, the heron's birthplace, acting as the link. We will take a look at writing a haiku with these three themes in mind later on.

Becoming the Object

A haiku is more than a description by someone looking at a scene, however. The writer of the haiku is trying (not usually consciously) to write from inside the subject, getting into the animal or insect or scenery that he or she is describing.

As Bashō said, "In writing, do not let a hair's breath separate yourself from the subject." This may sound like a very difficult thing to do, but really all that is necessary is to get the "everyday" you to step aside and let the scene you are describing take over. For example, if you are looking at a bear in a zoo, the "everyday you" might says things like "what would it be like to be a bear?" or "I feel the bear is lonely" or "I think it is mean to keep the bear in a cage." If, however, you just describe what you see and not what you think or feel, you will find that there is nothing separating you and the bear. You will have no problem expressing the "bearness" of the scene.

Haiku are rarely written from the imagination. "You can learn about the pine only from the pine, and about the bamboo only from the bamboo," said Bashō. A haiku poet looks at the subject that has caught their interest with great concentration and focuses on the reality that he or she sees.

Anywhere and everywhere one can be inspired to write a haiku . . . the first snowfall, mushrooms (or worms) springing up after a heavy rain, or even smoke from a factory chimney.

Haiku:

Haiku are for Sharing Experiences

When you are moved by something you see (or smell, or taste, or touch, or hear) and you want to tell someone about it, if you put a description of what your senses are telling you into haiku form, you will have written a haiku.

When you feel something very strongly, often you may not want to say a whole lot. In fact, maybe all you can do at first is hold your breath in amazement, or let out a big sigh, or a big shout. If you can write haiku, you can put a powerful moment like that into ordinary everyday words so that your moment becomes everyone's moment.

Haiku are always about what is happening to you "now," not something you remembered, or something you fantasized, or even something you dreamed of, but something that has caught your attention and is interesting to you, something that makes you stop. So haiku are always written in the present tense. People who read your haiku will know that you are describing something that you were looking at right then and there, as the words for the haiku popped into your mind. Because you are aiming to express things clearly, you can share the moment.

To Sum up so Far

(i)   A haiku in Japanese is usually divided into three groups of syllables (5-7-5), the first with five syllables, the second with seven and the last with five. Later, we will discuss why English translations have fewer syllables than they do in Japanese. For the moment, if you are going to try to write a haiku, you can try either 5-7-5 syllables (making 17 in all) or about 10 to 12 syllables, as haiku in English are often written.

(ii)   A haiku is concerned with a single happening that is being described in the present tense.

(iii) You will notice that all the haiku I have quoted so far are about nature: the frog in the old pond, the skinny frog, cherry blossoms, and the radish farmer in his field. Until recently, most haiku indicated which season they had been written in, and we will soon discuss the ''seasonal'' words used by Japanese haiku poets.

(iv)   A haiku is usually about two or more things we do not usually think of together. Associating them makes the person who reads the haiku say ''Wow'' or feel sad or happy or lonely, whether the poet intended it or not.

(v)   Although a haiku describes a scene, it should also allow the reader to feel some of the feelings the poet felt as he or she wrote the haiku. Maybe the reader will even find that the haiku has stirred up some of his or her own feelings. The best haiku will often leave you pondering some big thoughts, such as ''What does life mean?'' and ''Why am I here on earth?''

Let's Catch Our Breath

Although you now know some of the rules of writing haiku and have perhaps tried to write one, you may have also realized that people don't actually write haiku. "Wait a minute," you will say, "Isn't this book all about writing haiku?" Well, yes it is, and if you have read carefully what has been written so far, you will begin to see that it is the haiku that will do the writing, not you. The haiku will knock you over and come bursting out of your heart because you cannot stop it.

For your next haiku, go outdoors and walk around the yard, or up and down the street, or over to the park and back. Maybe only part of the haiku will hit you . . . "children laughing," "a bench with graffiti on it," "a cyclist whizzing past." Don't worry, later you can build up your haiku from these images that have captured you. And if too many words flood into your mind, then just cut them down like we did before.

Of course you want your haiku to be fresh and original – a clever new way of looking at something – but don't work too hard at being clever and original. Your early attempts are bound to sound like haiku you have read somewhere else, but if you have really been affected by what you have seen, heard, smelled, tasted or touched, you will find yourself saying it in your own style. You will be describing the moment as if you had never seen things quite that way before.

Haiku:

Japanese Haiku

◾

Besides learning all the regular subjects like math and history, Japanese students are also taught how to write haiku at school. Because Japan has had such a long history, every student is expected to know something about a great many historical events. So if a name, for example Yoshitsune, was used in a traditional haiku, everyone would know who was being referred to (in this case a famous warrior) and it wouldn't have to be explained. The same would be true if words from Japanese culture were used, words such as "Yoshino" (an area where many people go to look at the cherry trees in bloom) or "visiting graves" (which happens at *Obon*, an important summer festival, when families visit their ancestors' graves to honor the dead).

A Japanese haiku poet writing 300 or 400 years ago would also have been expected to know something about Chinese history, as well as Chinese paintings and literature, because much of Japanese culture came from China. A particular word used in a haiku might depend on everyone knowing what Chinese poem or piece of writing was being talked about.

If you are the butterfly
I am surely Chuang Tzu
dreaming.

In this haiku by Bashō, he is referring to Chuang Tzu, a Chinese follower of Taoism. Chuang Tzu woke from a dream of being a butterfly and wondered whether he was a man who had dreamed he was a butterfly, or a butterfly who was now dreaming he was a man.

one breath poetry

Since educated Japanese also know something of the basic religious and moral systems of Japan: Shintoism, Confucianism, Taoism and Buddhism, they would have no problem catching any reference to them in a haiku such as the next one by Chiyo-ni. Chiyo-ni, a female poet, was asked by her Zen teacher to convey the Buddhist idea that all the universe, in all the forms it has taken, came from a single concept – the void, the universal storehouse. She used a parallel idea of many gourds coming from a single plant.

A hundred gourds . . .
from a single creeper
grow.

A Taoist idea is that the world is always changing: as John Blofield, the Buddhist scholar, says, "loss, decay and death are just as natural as gain, growth and life." In spite of everything being subject to change, any detail at any moment can reveal the basic truths of the universe. That is also the essence of the haiku, where a simple everyday scene or object can open up to make you feel connected to the whole universe.

We said earlier that, besides letting the haiku answer the three questions what, when and where, haiku poets often try to name an object that is everlasting, one that is passing and something that links the two. This linking of the everyday passing scene with something that is universal is a Buddhist idea as well as a Taoist one. We will take a look at writing a haiku with this in mind later, but for now consider this haiku by Bashō.

> *Soon to die,*
> *but not knowing it . . .*
> *the cicadas sing.*

yagate shinu / *keshiki wa*   *mie-zu*   / *semi no koe*
Soon die   / sign   not able to see / cicada's voices

Here, the Buddhist notion of change is contrasted with the worldly careless chirps of the cicadas, unaware that they will soon die.

Bashō and other haiku poets were students of Zen Buddhism. Zen is a way of finding answers to the mystery of the universe by looking within oneself. While Zen students sit in silent meditation, a Zen insight can also be experienced by just carrying on everyday activities like washing the dishes or tidying your room. Zen Buddhism connects small moments of life to the whole universe and so, like Taoism, its study is perfect for someone who wants to write haiku. It encourages a very simple lifestyle closely connected to nature and the seasons.

one breath poetry

Between the Lines

Let's see what else makes haiku a particularly Japanese kind of poetry. Japanese people use words sparingly; they often don't finish their sentences because they know that the person they are talking to will understand what the end of the sentence will be. That is because the Japanese are bound very closely together by a long and strong culture. They can easily guess what the other person means, and so they don't have to spell everything out. For example, instead of saying, "Well, I'd rather not do this right now" when requested to do something they don't want to do, a Japanese will reply, "*Chotto* . . ." meaning "Well . . ." and the requester will understand that he or she doesn't want to do what has been asked and is refusing in a vague and roundabout way.

Because Japanese society (unlike many countries) is not multicultural, the Japanese all share similar customs and ways of looking at things. So, in order to be understood by fellow Japanese, they merely have to hint at what they are trying to say. Such hinting is perfect for writing haiku, where, although the scene must be clear, there must be so much left unsaid. This is not just because the haiku is short but also because the experience that triggers the haiku is often too deep and too difficult to put into words.

Japanese rarely use "I," "you" or "we," so you will seldom find many pronouns in Japanese haiku. On the whole, Japanese like to give facts without emotions, which makes writing haiku much easier for them. Haiku poets don't write things like "It was so lovely," "It was cute," "I hated it." There is a Japanese quotation, *kami nagara no michi*, that means things should be left to the will of the gods; the Japanese do not like to interfere in situations where we might rush in and think we are helping. This is because they accept the way life goes more easily than we do. *Shiyō ga nai* (it can't be helped) is a common expression. So in their haiku you won't find them saying, "this is bad and must be

Haiku:

stopped'' and ''that is good and must be encouraged.'' They just describe a scene and leave all the judgment making to other cultures that are more judgmental. Ugly and distasteful subjects are just as valid for Japanese haiku as are cherry blossoms and the harvest moon, as in this haiku by Tōta.

> *The factory that fires workers*
> *also spews autumn-cloudy water*
> *into the canal.*

| *kubi kiru kōba* | / *shuudon-no   mizu o* | / *unga ni   haki* |
| worker firing factory | / autumn cloudy water | / canal into vomiting |

Because Japan is a very crowded country, Japanese people have learned to live in modest homes and to take pleasure in and cultivate the smallest things in nature, such as chrysanthemums, morning glories and *bonsai* (miniature trees). Attitudes are changing and this may not be true about the young people of Japan today, but it is certainly true of their parents. Giving attention to small everyday things is a perfect way of behaving for haiku writers, who use these small daily events as triggers for haiku that can reveal deep truths.

Kireji, Cutting Words

Most Japanese haiku are still written with 5-7-5 *onji*, which I will talk about soon. They also contain *kireji* (e.g., *ya*, *kana*, *keri*, *yara*, *yo*, *zo*, *koso*, *to*), cutting words that indicate pauses. Because we don't have such words in English, we use punctuation marks such as commas, colons and semicolons to show where we would like the reader to pause.

Kireji are also used to give certain words emphasis. The following are some frequently used cutting words.

ya   can usually be represented as either ":" or "!" and is often followed by a description of what went before it or a new topic, and so is used to divide the haiku.

kana   is like a deep sigh and can be shown in English as "Ah!" "*Kana*" usually occurs at the end of a haiku to show the reader that, although the emotion the poet feels isn't spelled out, he or she wants the reader to know it is strong, as in this haiku by Yasui.

I know the wild-geese
        ate the barley, yet
                when they fly away . . .

mugi kuishi / *kari*   *to* *omoedo*   / *wakare kana*
barley ate   / wild-geese in this way think / parting kana

Yasui knows the geese are bad because they destroy the barley, but he wants very much to forgive them because when they fly away they are so beautiful. And so he finishes the haiku with *kana*!

Haiku:

Keri (which we have already met) is used when a pause is needed and also to emphasize the previous word, usually a verb. In English, *keri* is often indicated by "...").

Yara is used when an English speaker would say "I wonder" and indicates a pause for reflection. The poet probably doesn't expect an answer.

To is used when we would write "in this way someone spoke or acted" and it is also used for listing things, as in Ryōta's haiku, which follows.

Yo, zo and *koso* all emphasize the previous word or words.

all were silent . . .
the guest, the host
and the white chrysanthemum.

mono-iwazu	/ *kyaku to*	*teishu to*	/ *shiragiku*	*to*
not saying anything	/ guest and host and		/ white chrysanthemum and	

The white chrysanthemum is often used in haiku as a symbol for Buddha and his laws.

Look at the haiku you have already written and see if you have included moments for pausing and thinking, using punctuation as a substitute for these "cutting words."

one breath poetry

The Seasonal Word

Japanese haiku, even today, usually have a seasonal word (*kigo*) or some reference to nature in them. These seasonal words were originally used to date the *renga* (a long poem in which sets of three lines developed, over time, into the haiku). Later it became automatic to use seasonal words. Japan is a small country and even though the seasons vary from north to south, many people understand which season is being talked about just by the mention of a seasonal word. To Japanese, seasonal words don't just suggest the season, they are the season:

Spring
melting snow
plum blossom
cherry blossom
tea picking
skylark
nightingale
returning geese
butterflies
azaleas

Summer
waterfall
rice paddies
fan
mosquitoes
cuckoo
frog
magnolia
cicada
fireflies

Autumn
starry night
harvest moon
colored leaves
rice cutting
loneliness
deer
dragonfly
chrysanthemum
mushrooms

Winter
snow
charcoal fire
radish pulling
bears
eagle
twigs
pine
quilted clothes
withered plants

Haiku writers in Japan can buy books that list seasonal words, and often they will find more than 1,000 listed. One such book (published in 1927) had 4,300 seasonal words listed, which goes to show how sensitive Japanese people used to be to nature.

Haiku:

Even today, Japanese continue to use seasonal words in their haiku because it links them to hundreds of years of haiku writing. Although most people in Japan now live in cities, they are still fond of nature. You continue to see many homes with a *bonsai* collection outside and some *ikebana* (formal flower arrangements) inside, and people still take the time to go and view the first plum and cherry blossoms in spring, or sit on the veranda (or balcony more likely) to view the autumn moon.

Why don't we stop here for a moment to make seasonal word lists with the feelings you associate with each season. For example, spring: newborn lambs, joy, hope; summer: fullness, mosquitoes (irritation); autumn: red maple leaves, sadness, decay; winter: snowfall, loneliness, death and sleep.

Try to write a haiku about each season, using at least one of the words you have listed in each haiku. Of course, it is agreed that remembering a season is not as good as describing the current season, so I expect that the haiku about the present season will be the most pleasing.

Special Ideas

To write a traditional Japanese haiku, you must not only be familiar with words and feelings that the Japanese have associated with each season. There are also some special, and rather difficult, ideas that Japanese people appreciate when they are looking at art, reading poetry or listening to Japanese music.

Sabi   A word that describes beauty that has a touch of loneliness about it.

Aware   A sadness because everything in life must pass away.

Wabi   The appreciation of simple everyday things and how they can reveal the eternal.

Yugen   The ability to glimpse the eternal in a world that is constantly changing, a sensing of the mystery of life.

These words all describe qualities that the Japanese appreciate in their haiku.

Japanese haiku do not rhyme, but they often contain puns, which can make them difficult to translate. It is easy to pun in Japanese since many words have the same pronunciation. For example, the sound *kan* can mean "government," "midwinter" and "coffin," as well as 40 other different words!

Traditional Images

Usually you will find two or more images in a Japanese haiku. One image will not describe the other, but the two images will be connected, often in a way that you will have to intuit. Take a look at the images of the old pond and the frog in the Bashō haiku quoted at the beginning of the book and the images of the crow and evening in the one below, also by Bashō.

On a bare branch
a crow has settled . . .
autumn evening.

| *Kare eda   ni* | / | *karasu no tomari keri* | / | *aki no kure* |
| bare branch on | / | crow   has perched | / | autumn nightfall |

How are they connected? Did you notice the "cutting word," *keri*, that was used to separate the two images from the third?

From all the things we have talked about that Japanese people are expected to know, you can see that you would have to do quite a bit of studying before being able to write a traditional Japanese haiku. But even if you can't read Japanese, and know little about Japanese and Chinese culture and history, you can still write haiku. Haiku have the power to intensify and make objects important and that can be done in English or Japanese, or any other language.

one breath poetry

Haiku:

Haiku in English

In textbooks, haiku are usually written in the 5-7-5 syllable form; but as you can see from some of the translations we have given, 17 syllables sometimes seem too many for an English haiku. This is because the Japanese 5-7-5 pattern is not actually made up of syllables, as we know them, but rather of *onji*. *Onji* (Japanese syllables) are very short, either a single vowel (*a*); one or two consonants + a vowel (*ku*, *chi*); or the letter "n" when not followed by a vowel.

There are no diphthongs in Japanese, so a double vowel counts as two *onji*: e.g., *jūdō* – ju-u-do-o (four *onji*). A double consonant also counts as two *onji*: e.g., *Nippon* (the word the Japanese use for Japan) has four *onji*, Ni-p-po-n. A more extreme example is the Japanese word for blue, *aoi* (a-o-i), which has three *onji*, compared with the following English words, which each contain only one syllable: *a*, *at*, *two*, *four*, *might* and *strike*. These examples should convince you that Japanese *onji* are, on average, much shorter than English syllables.

Some writers feel that 17 English syllables are fine. But other writers feel that 10 to 12 English syllables better approximates the 17 *onji* found in traditional Japanese haiku. Too few syllables don't suit the Western style of poetry. Perhaps the best would be to aim for three short lines, the second one being a little longer.

Once more,
the tree's bare branches . . .
melting snow.

one breath poetry

Try writing a haiku with a 5-7-5 syllable pattern and see how you feel about it. Some people feel it links them to the long line of Japanese haiku poets, but does it really? What do you feel? Go back and check some of your earlier haiku. Can you make them closer to 10 syllables long and still keep the image clear? How about keeping to the ''one-breath'' concept for your haiku?

Haiku:

More on Images

As we mentioned in the section on Japanese haiku, the best haiku seem to take two rather different things and relate them. One of the two objects could be close up and one far away, or one small and one very big:

Misty sky,
fresh paint on the balcony . . .
endless grey.

Carpeted room:
sound of crimson nails
pounding the keys.

It is not just enough to mention two (or more things); they must relate in some way. In the first poem, the two greys hit me, and I created a rather sad scene. In the second, two textures are put side by side: the soft thick carpet, probably pale brown, contrasting with the sharp brittle painted nails. Such images, put together in this way, give rise to new ways of looking at what you are describing. In the haiku about the host, the guest and the chrysanthemum (page 19), the three objects were linked because they were all silent, but that silence could give rise to the idea that silence is both empty and, at the same time, full. And that is really something to think about!

As was mentioned earlier (page 14), it has been suggested that one of the subjects of a haiku should reflect permanence. For example, in Bashō's poem about the frog, this would be "old pond." The second subject should represent something that passes, as life does; for example, "the frog jumping." The third line should link the two. In this haiku, the link is "the sound of water." A perfect haiku!

Here is a haiku by 11-year-old Chris Hillbruner of the United States, which really speaks of permanence and decay:

> *The damp forest floor*
> *smelling of fresh pine needles*
> *and old rotting logs.*

Maybelle Suarez of British Columbia, Canada, wrote this haiku when she was in Grade 6. It also has the elements of permanence and passing things:

> *Face from the water*
> *Looking back at me, wrinkled*
> *By touch of my hand.*

The timeless quality of a pool is contrasted with the "wrinkles" that must happen to all of us. These two images are linked by the phrase "touch of my hand."

And here is a haiku written by students Rody Turpijn and Michiel van Rossum from the Netherlands, which literally joins the universal to the everyday:

*Star in the universe
the earth in the galaxy
and me in my home.*

Although a haiku should have two or more images, it should only be about one event, one moment when you sensed something and stopped and drew a breath.

You may have noticed that in the haiku presented so far there are no metaphors or similes. The words "like a" or "as" should not be used in haiku. You see, if you say something is like something else, for example, "a girl is like a rose," you are no longer talking about the girl. Your ideas have gone to roses and everything that we associate with them. In this way, similes take you outside the experience by comparing the object to something that is not present at the moment the haiku has occurred to you.

We cannot say often enough that if the image that stirred up the emotion is clear, then the emotion will be clear to the reader. You are sharing the feeling by sharing the image that triggered the feeling. Don't tell the reader what to feel, tell the image and let it cook in the reader's own mind. Don't say, "How sad!" Show what is sad. Haiku happen when you are so full of what you have seen, heard, tasted, smelled or touched that the words just tumble out when you try to tell your friends about it. So haiku help by making you able to share a very deep experience, even though a lot of it stays unspoken. At least you have shared the "what" that started the feeling inside you.

The more you write from your own experience, the better the haiku will be. If your experience is real, your words will also be real, otherwise you will just be playing with words, which is fine, but it doesn't make a haiku. Don't set out to write a haiku just because you want to write a good haiku. When you start out having had an interesting and intense experience (no matter how small) you stand a good chance of writing a good haiku anyway, as sixth-grader Nicole Fuger (George Hilliard School, Kamloops, B.C., Canada) did when she noticed her bedspread.

The color of sun
It brightens up the whole room
My yellow bedspread.

Here Nicole has taken an image that struck her and used another pleasant form of haiku that gives image, image and surprise. You may wonder which is the best sequence for the images of your poem. Try starting your haiku with the object that first hits your senses and leave the surprise connection to the last line the way Nicole did. Write some more haiku using this form and see if the last line doesn't make you smile with satisfaction.

Samādhi

Sometimes haiku will take a small event like petals falling and will open in front of you the ideas of life and death and the inevitability of change. The very best haiku are written from a state of samādhi (*sammai* in Japanese), which occurs when the haiku poet and his subject become one, as we spoke about at the beginning of the book when you and the bear became one. In archery, the archer, his bow, arrow and target must become one for the archer to hit his target. This united state is called samādhi. If we want to hit the target in writing haiku, we also need to be in a state of samādhi. This is a very deep experience and is hard to describe, but I believe that most people have felt it sometime in their lives. Perhaps you were out fishing with your father and the sunset was perfect, or maybe one night the moonlight flooded your room so that you felt you could dissolve in it. Moments like these can lead to a state of complete concentration and from this may come a flash of *satori* (a deep understanding of the universe). In this haiku, the poet Chiyo must have had just such an experience:

Calling Cuckoo, Cuckoo
All night long
until the dawn.

hototogisu   /   hototogisu tote   /   ake ni keri
cuckoo   /   cuckoo saying   /   the end keri

Chiyo, a nun, had stayed up all night trying to describe the sound of the cuckoo. She couldn't seem to find the right words. At last, almost as the sun began to rise, the words above came to her. In the end, all she could say was the call of the bird, but doesn't it seem just right?

Pauses and Editing

Do you remember the "cutting words" that Japanese use, *kireji*? Pauses such as these "cutting words" help you contrast, compare or relate the two or more topics you are using in your haiku. How can we best imitate *kireji* in English? Reread the pages on "cutting words" in the Japanese haiku section (page 18). To refresh this idea, write another haiku and concentrate on the punctuation that we can use to imitate the job those "cutting words" do.

Keep your haiku spontaneous and keep them simple. Don't think "simple" comes easily; most haiku writers have spent, and still spend, a lot of time revising their haiku until the poem feels just right. The essence of haiku is the immediate response; any editing can come later. Bashō said the poem should be written as swiftly as a woodcutter fells a tree, or a swordsman leaps at a dangerous enemy.

In Bashō's frog poem, the sound of the splash and the image of a frog jumping in the water came to Bashō first. He didn't immediately think of a first line. One of his students suggested *yamabuki*, a bright yellow wild rose bush, but that made the poem very light and springlike. Bashō hadn't felt that way, and so he waited for the first line that he thought most appropriate. Only later did he add "an old pond," which he thought made just the right beginning for the haiku. This creates a much darker and perhaps sadder picture.

By the way, before Bashō wrote that haiku, frogs were only mentioned in Japanese poetry because of the croaks they made. This time, however, it was the frog's movement that attracted attention and triggered the haiku.

Haiku:

Leave It Out

What to leave out? Most adjectives, adverbs and even a few prepositions! You are describing an ordinary experience that you have just realized is a "wow" one, so use ordinary words and above all no emotional words, no "lovely," "beautiful," "cute" or "horrible"! Eliminate "I" since you don't need it to show what you are feeling. Take out as many "the's" and "a's" as you can.

Here is a charming haiku by Logan Balser of Canada (written when he was 12) that would have been much stronger without the word "lovely."

Green morning marvel!
lovely nameless little hill
on a sea of mist.

Japanese haiku rarely present a whole sentence. Just like the Japanese, you don't need to say everything. Let the person who will read your haiku have a chance to imagine just what you saw and felt. Bashō said that showing 70 to 80 percent of a subject is good, but people never tire of reading haiku that only show 50 to 60 percent. Sometimes Japanese haiku are so vague it is difficult to really decide what the subject is. Suggest, but make it enough to give a clear picture.

We have talked about cutting out unnecessary words, but taking it to an extreme, someone once said that haiku is the poetry of nouns! It would be hard to write a haiku consisting of nothing but nouns, but try writing a haiku with no verbs like the following two haiku by Bashō. In these haiku, the verbs are just implied.

The usually hateful crow
now so different
on the morn of snow!

> *Higoro   nikumu / karasu mo   yuki no / ashita kana*
> Usually hateful   / crow even snow's / morning kana

Of course,"now so different" really means, "now seems so different." Here Bashō is contrasting the crow, which he usually dislikes, with a transformed crow when seen against the background of snow. Haiku are very much about seeing everyday things in a different light. This poem has 18 *onji*, which was very unusual at that time.

Here is another verbless haiku:

A cloud of cherry blossom,
a temple bell . . .
Ueno? Asakusa?

> *Hana no   kumo / kane wa   Ueno ka / Asakusa ka*
> Blossom's cloud / bell   Ueno?   / Asakusa?

Bashō is saying that amidst the cherry blossom he hears a temple bell. Is it the one at Ueno or the one at Asakusa? The haiku sits very well without the verbs, though.

Forms For Haiku

Haiku in English are not always written with three non-rhyming lines. Back to Bashō's pond. Here is a translation by Daisetz Suzuki. Notice that because he wants to keep the feeling of the Japanese form, he does not use 5-7-5 English syllables.

The old pond, ah!
a frog jumps in:
the water's sound!

Originally in Japan, a haiku was written in one line from the top to the bottom of the paper, or if there was a painting with the haiku, the line might run diagonally. Let's see how this works with Bashō's frog. This is how David G. Lanoue translates it:

old
pond
a
frog
jumps
in
water
sound

When you write it this way you can really test for the importance of each word. How are you going to make each word count? Rewrite the haiku you have already written so one word stands under another. Do the words still seem as suitable? If not, change them.

In English, poets have written haiku in several forms, including:

Three lines with the first and third line rhyming
Two lines that rhyme
Four lines with the second and fourth line rhyming, or
Four non-rhyming lines:

old pool . . .
the frog jumps,
sound of water cool.

> *Old pond: a frog bounds*
> *into it . . .the water's sound.*

An old pond . . .
when a frog bounds
into it —
water's sound

> *The old pond . . .*
> *its silence broken*
> *as a frog jumps in*
> *with a splash*

Some of these are terribly wordy and perhaps not really true to the original haiku, but I included them to illustrate the many ways that non-Japanese-speaking poets have chosen to present their haiku translations.

There are big discussions between non-Japanese haiku poets as to whether lines should rhyme or not. Rhyme usually closes a poem but haiku are open, leaving you wondering or questioning. Rhyme often distracts from the meaning of the haiku and makes it sound too much like a TV jingle. By looking for a rhyming word, you might not be able to use another word that would be very strong and much more appropriate. But if a rhyme just happens and it doesn't seem too noticeable, why not leave it in?

Haiku:

Thoughts After Reading Haiku

Haiku are meant to be presented in one breath, but the feelings and ideas that they give rise to should increase on each re-reading. If a haiku can be just read and the reader feels "well that's nice" but it doesn't bring up deeper emotions in him or her, then it is not a good haiku. A good haiku sets you thinking, often about things that you may not usually wonder about.

Reread the haiku of Bashō's frog jumping in the pond. What do you feel after you read it? What sort of thoughts come into your mind? The old pond could make one think of how tranquil situations can be disturbed, but how the disturbance doesn't last long. Or you might think about how the tranquillity of the pond was broken by the sound; but was it the sound of the water or the sound of the frog jumping into the water that was heard? Does the pond make you think of tadpoles you collected in the spring? Or perhaps Bashō was mistaken and there was no old pond, no frog, and the sound was of something else. What could it have been? And that is often how haiku affect you. They leave you asking questions.

There are often many opinions as to the meaning of a good haiku. However, it is not necessary to analyze a haiku as we have just done, or even give it a title. A haiku is a haiku and is to be experienced and enjoyed, not investigated.

one breath poetry   37

Although we have just said that haiku needn't be explained, it is sometimes interesting to know the circumstances in which a haiku was written. The following story may not be true, but it was said that Bashō was once asked to write a haiku about the eight famous views that people admired around Lake Biwa. Bashō knew that at one time this had been done in a *tanka* (early form of Japanese poetry) of 31 syllables, but to do it in a haiku of 17 *onji* would be impossible, so Bashō wrote:

*Seven views
were hidden in mist, but
Mii's bell was heard.*

| *shichi kei wa* | / *kiri ni kakurete* | / *Mii no kane* |
| seven views | / mist concealed | / Mii's bell |

(Mii temple was one of the eight famous views.)

A good haiku raises many questions, but within the haiku there should be no logical deductions or conclusions such as, "then it's true that," or "this happened because of that." However, even though we hope that whoever reads our haiku is left with questions, we trust they won't ask "What does the poem mean?" The best reaction is that they just smile or nod, silently agreeing that your way of expressing the scene (and indirectly your feelings) really was successful. People don't like to tell a joke and then have to explain it; it's the same with haiku.

Haiku:

Haiku and the Senses

Haiku are written because we see, hear, touch, taste or smell something. Haiku come from the senses. How many senses are mentioned in this haiku by Bashō?

Ki no moto ni   / *shiru mo*   *namasu mo*   /   *sakura kana*
tree under   / soup also fish salad also   / cherry blossom!

Under the cherry tree,
soup, fish and salad
spiced with cherry blossoms!

And how about in
this one by Sogetsu?

As the festival dancing dies,
the sound of the wind in the pine trees
and the insects' voices.

Bon-odori   / *ato*   *wa*   *matsu – kaza*   / *mushi no koe*
Obon dancing   / after   pine tree wind   / insects'   voices

Obon is a summer festival when the spirits of dead loved ones return. It is a great time for feasting and dancing before the spirits are speeded on their way back to the other side.

one breath poetry

Louise Baozhen Huang, a Singapore student, wrote these three strong images to give her haiku (covering several senses) a definite feeling of the countryside:

Buttercups in bloom
shredded cheese on lettuce leaves
on blue table-cloth.

Grade 6 student Yukiko Shinpo of Japan really triggers the senses with this noisy, colorful haiku.

Sunflowers
and the sun yelling
together

hi ma wari to   /   taiyo isshoni   /   koe o dasu
sunflowers and   /   sun   together /   call out

And here is another for the senses written by 12-year-old Anne-Claire Morel from France:

In these summer months
will sparrows leave one cherry
for me to nibble?

Write a haiku being very aware of the senses. Can you get all five senses in one haiku? It may not be a very satisfactory haiku, but it would be fun to try. Perhaps you will use a trick the way Bashō did in his haiku of the eight famous views of Lake Biwa.

Do Haiku Ever Tell Stories?

The inspiration for haiku come from brief moments, so they cannot be said to tell stories. Sometimes the images used are so strong, however, that a storyline almost leaps out at you from the haiku, as in this poem by Buson.

A night's shelter!
he demands, and throws down his sword . . .
the snow blows in.

| *yado-kase* | *to* | / | *katana nagedasu* | / | *fubuki kana* |
| give accommodation | | / | so sword throws down | / | blown snow kana |

Who is demanding a night's shelter? A robber? A samurai? A traveller? And what is it all about? It is as if the man, the sword and the snow have all been blown in together.

Here is a haiku written by 12-year-old Monisa Nandi of Hong Kong:

The sun is setting
two rabbits sit in a field
waiting for the moon

A good beginning for a fairy story! Try writing a samurai story and a fairy story using the above haiku as a starting point. Then write a story-suggesting-haiku yourself.

one breath poetry

41

Translating Anybody?

I know that most readers of this book neither speak nor read Japanese. I also know that most haiku poets would frown and shake their heads at my suggestion, but why don't you try to translate a Japanese haiku anyway? I will give you the words to one of Issa's haiku; you put them into your own words in a haiku form of your choice. Later, when you come to read about Issa, you will see how it could be translated.

yuki tokete   /   mura   ippai-no   /   kodomo kana
snow melting / village full of   /   children *kana*

(For *kana*, check the ''cutting word'' section on page 18.)

Haiku:

Putting it all Together

To review, a haiku describes one event, is in the present tense and refers to an image(s) somehow connected to nature. A haiku is about something that the poet has noticed, heard, smelled, tasted or touched. The poet makes that moment, however small, a very important one. In Japanese, the haiku usually has 17 *onji*; in English, aim to begin with a short line, followed by a slightly longer line, and finish with a short line, altogether around 10 to 12 syllables. When you read about the history of haiku (in the next chapter), you will learn that from time to time poets stuck too closely to the rules and the haiku had no spontaneity. So remember, these guidelines are just guidelines. You can choose to stay inside them or not, so long as your haiku has "heart."

Haiku:

The History of Haiku

■

These words are a summary of the history of haiku and are used by students to remind themselves of how haiku came about. Besides a brief account of each, we will also look at the lives of Japan's leading haiku poets.

The very first kinds of poems in Japan were called *katauta*. They were really questions and answers between man and the gods and were about 17 to 19 *onji* long. By 700-1100 C.E., when the emperor's court was situated at Heiankyo (or Kyoto as it is called today), the emperor and his court nobles loved to write short poems called *tanka*. In fact, the better a poet you were, the more distinguished a noble you were thought to be. Of course, the emperor was always said to be the best poet, even if he couldn't write very well at all. Even today in Japan, the emperor has a haiku party at New Year, and everyone in Japan is invited to send in his or her very best haiku. The emperor is expected to write one also, although it is never judged.

People at the Heian court wrote *tanka* more often than we write letters today. They wrote poetry in spring to praise the first blossoms, and they wrote poetry in summer as they listened to the insects cries. In autumn, when the leaves of the maple turned crimson and the courtiers gathered to watch the harvest moon, they wrote poems, as they did in winter, when they sat looking out at the deep snow. Of course, if they were in love, many *tanka* were sent back and forth between the lovers. Even a poem before dying was expected; we will show you some later on. Instead of pointing out something that had interested them, courtiers might recite a poem instead.

Because everything was very elegant at the Heian court, these small poems were very popular. *Tanka* have five lines, containing in turn 5-7-5-7-7 *onji* each. Very refined people were not expected to spell everything out, and so those poems were only suggestions of scenes and ideas.

By the 17th century, groups of poets would write poetry together, linking these *tanka*. One poet would make up the 5-7-5 *onji* part and another would add the 7-7 *onji* part. The 7-7 *onji* would then suggest a 5-7-5 *onji*, so that one verse led to another, but there was no story or central idea. Sometimes poets would join as many as 100 verses, and the whole poem was called a *renga*. The starting three lines of the *renga* was called *hokku*, and it was always written by the most distinguished poet present. It was so important that often poets would prepare *hokku* before the poetry meeting in case they were asked to start. The *hokku* always had to contain a word to show the season in which it was written (to date it), and also some kind of exclamatory word, much as we would use an exclamation mark.

After some years, many rules came to be adopted regulating how to write these linked verses (*renga*). So many rules, in fact, that almost all originality disappeared and poetry writing of this kind became like a game you played with friends. Rules became totally ridiculous, such as the one stating that if the 5-7-5 part of the *renga* mentioned the first month of the year, then the 7-7 part had to also and the next 5-7-5 part had to mention spring, and so on. Poetry writing became very complex, and it was hard to express true spontaneous feelings.

46   *Haiku:*

The *renga* were of two kinds: serious, reflective ones using the language of the courtiers and those using the speech and idioms of ordinary people, often witty and vulgar (*haikai no renga* meaning playful linked poems). The latter were often written by young poets who got bored with all the rules, and they were usually very amusing. Poets would often write them as they relaxed after a *tanka* poetry contest. *Haikai no renga* freed *renga* from the formal speech of the court. Eventually, people such as Bashō often just quoted the first three lines, the *hokku*, and so the haiku was born.

Bashō

Bashō (Matsuo Kinsaku), the poet who wrote about the frog jumping into the old pond, lived from 1644 to 1694. To make a parallel with a Western poet of comparable stature, William Shakespeare died about 30 years before Bashō was born.

Bashō was born near Ueno in Iga Province. He was the son of a lower-ranking samurai. While young he entered the service of Tōdō Yoshitada, the son of a local warlord. They became close companions. As samurai were no longer involved in major wars, since the country was now unified, they turned to practicing the fine arts as well as martial skills.

Bashō and Yoshitada learned to write poetry. When Yoshitada died at a young age, Bashō was very sad and left Ueno to live in Kyoto and then later in Edo (Tokyo). He had already begun to write poetry and haiku, and soon began to judge haiku competitions and to have many students. For a while he lived in a small hut in the grounds of one of his student's homes. Around the hut his students planted banana trees (bashō) and so Bashō's small home was called Bashō-an (Banana Hermitage) and that is how he adopted his pen name.

In 1681, he wrote the haiku about a crow settling on the bare branch (page 23). This poem marked the beginning of Bashō's particular style of writing haiku. Reread it. It is natural writing, with no puns or fancy words. The two parts, the crow and the autumn evening, exist on their own; they are not linked by simile

48

Haiku:

or metaphor, as they might be in Western poetry, and yet they are wonderfully joined by the sadness of the scene. The poem has great depth since it raises questions such as "Is Bashō comparing the way that nightfall settles with the way that crow settles?" "Which is blacker, the night or the crow?" "Is the day coming to a close reminding us that the year is also coming to an end, as must our own lives?" and so on.

Bashō was also famous for the *renga* that he wrote with groups of his friends and students (Bashō popularized the 36-linked verse form known as *kasen*). He changed the *renga* so it was no longer just linked verses but had a harmony of feeling that gave the verses a unity.

It was also Bashō who freed the first three lines of the *renga* to make them a poem in their own right, the *hokku*. The first three lines of the renga anticipated a further verse, but the *hokku* (the word haiku was first used with frequency by Shiki, a later haiku poet) stood on its own. Bashō's *hokku* revealed the universal truths behind everyday images and so gave those three lines of verse great importance. The poet no longer just painted a scene, but by becoming one with his subject, he could reveal a truth common to everything.

Bashō was very critical of most haiku that were being written. He said that if you wrote five haiku in your life you were a haiku writer, but if you wrote 10, you were a master. Of course he wasn't just talking about everyday haiku, but haiku that are so perfect they really take your breath away. Actually, Bashō wrote over 1,000 haiku in his lifetime.

Bashō was a student of Zen Buddhism, although he never became a monk. In Zen Buddhism you meditate on an object until you become one with that object and that is just what Bashō said you had to do to write a good haiku. Right at the beginning of this book we quoted him as saying, "In writing, do not let a hair's breath separate yourself from the subject." For haiku, instead of meditating as you would in Zen meditation, you concentrate on something that you have noticed so intensely that the whole or part of the haiku springs into your mind. Bashō wanted to identify with that "something." He was one of the most nature-oriented haiku poets.

For hundreds of years it had been considered good behaviour for a samurai, priest, monk or noble to leave a death poem. Often, to make sure it was good, people would prepare their death haiku long before they died. Here is Bashō's death poem:

Sick on a journey –
    dreams wander on
        over dried up fields

| *tabi ni yamite* | / *yume wa kare no wo* | / *kakemeguru* |
| journey on, becoming sick | / dreams, dried up fields on | / run about |

As I mentioned, Bashō had many followers who met and wrote *renga* together. They also sent their most recent *hokku* to one another. *Hokku* actually means "sending verse." Bashō loved to discuss poetry writing with his friends and students. He also loved to travel and later we will talk about the haiku he wrote in his travel diaries. In 1689, he took a long trip with his friend and student, Sora, and from that journey came the *haibun* (a travel diary containing haiku), *Narrow Road to the Interior*.

Haiku:

Buson

People began to imitate Bashō's haiku and different schools of haiku sprang up, each with their own rules such as the one that said no foreign words must be used. Once again, too many rules began to be introduced and that meant not enough real depth of feeling in the haiku.

There were, however, a few exceptions, and Taniguchi Buson (1715-1783), who lived about the time of Bach and Handel, was one. He is considered second only to Bashō as the greatest haiku poet. Buson was also famous as a painter of *haiga*, haiku illustrations. He not only painted *haiga* for his own haiku but also did some *haiga* for Bashō's haiku. Buson wrote 3,000 haiku in his lifetime. Here are a few:

In the spring rain:
talking to each other
go raincoat and umbrella.

harusame   ya / monogatari-yuku / mino   to   kasa
spring rain   / speaking   go   / raincoat and umbrella

(The *mino* was a straw raincoat worn by a man and the paper umbrella, in this case, was carried by a woman.)

The following poem contrasts the large bell and the delicate butterfly. Just as we do not know our future, the butterfly does not know that soon its sleep may be disturbed.

On the temple bell
a butterfly has settled
and is sleeping.

| *tsurigane-ni* | / *tomarite* | *nemuru* | / *kochō* | *kana* |
| temple bell on | / settling | sleep | / butterfly | ah! |

The next haiku suggests a double sadness:

For I who go,
for you who remain –
two autumns!

| *yuku* | *ware ni* | / *todomaru* | *nare* | *ni* | / *aki* | *futatsu* |
| going | I | / remain | you | | / autumns | two |

Buson was an observer of the world rather than a deeply spiritual person like Bashō, or a compassionate person like Issa, whom we will look at next. His haiku explore and enjoy the world and the beauty of women.

Haiku:

Issa

Issa (Yatarō Kobayashi) is probably the best loved of all haiku poets. Issa means "one cup of tea," and Issa compared his wandering life with the disappearance of the froth on a cup of Japanese tea. Issa lived from 1763 to 1827 (about the time of the Napoleonic wars). He was born in a mountain village in what is now Nagano Prefecture. He became a Buddhist priest and lived in great poverty. Issa called his broken-down house *kuzu-ya*, "trash house."

Issa's haiku are easy to understand because he didn't refer to Chinese poetry and Japanese and Chinese history as much as earlier haiku poets. Using everyday idioms and expressions, he wrote about beggars, lords, frogs and fleas, all with equal interest. Issa was a devout Buddhist and viewed everyday life as if it were Buddha's Heaven, in spite of the many tragedies in his life. His mother died when he was small; later his father remarried and his stepmother was unkind. He left home when he was 14. Once when his stepmother sent him to a village festival in shabby clothes and the other children wouldn't play with him, he wrote:

Come
orphan sparrow
and play with me.

Ore to   kite   / asobe yo oya no / nai suzume
Me with come / play orphan   / sparrow

He was said to be six at the time, but people now think this haiku was written many years later.

one breath poetry

When Issa married, all his own children died before they were one year old, except the child that was born after he died. In spite of all this sorrow, his poems saw beauty in all things. Issa fought for the underdog all his life as in his haiku about the skinny frog (page 2). Here is a haiku in which a nobleman is humbled:

A warlord
is made to get off his horse . . .
by cherry blossoms.

> *Daimyoo wo* / *uma kara orosu* / *sakura kana*
> daimyō / horse from bring down / cherry blossoms!

What a great surprise that third line is! Usually everyone had to bow down when the warlord passed. In this haiku, the warlord is humbled by the beauty of the cherry blossom and gets off his horse to admire it.

Snow melts
and the village is spilling over –
with children.

This is a translation of the haiku on page 42. Was your translation something like this?

Haiku:

Issa loved the unexpected: cherry blossoms stuck in the mud, snow melting and the village overflowing with children, a swallow flying out of the nose of the great statue of Buddha.

Issa wrote more than 2,000 haiku. This haiku is sometimes said to be Issa's death poem:

From washbasin
to washbasin drifting
nothing makes any sense.

tarai kara	/	*tarai ni utsuru*	/	*chinpunkan*
basin from	/	basin to drifting	/	nonsense

The basins are of course the one the newborn baby was washed in, and the one used for washing the corpse. *Chinpunkan* really means the unintelligible sound of a foreign language. As I mentioned earlier, poets didn't always write their death poem just before dying, and it is thought that Issa wrote this haiku earlier. His actual death poem found under his pillow was:

arigata	*ya*	/	*fusuma no*	*yuki*	*mo*	/	*Joodo*	*kara*
thanks due		/	bedding's	snow	also	/	Pure Land	from

Thankful because
the snow on the bedclothes
is also from Heaven.

Shiki

Noboru Masaoka (Shiki was a pen name meaning cuckoo) was a later writer (1867-1902). He was born about the time that the American commodore Matthew Perry and his black ships opened Japan to the West after it had been in seclusion for 300 years. Shiki at first became a reporter, but when he got tuberculosis he could not work and remained an invalid for the rest of his short life. In spite of his illness, he was able to reform the haiku movement.

Haiku writing had once more become full of rules and lacked passion and imagination, so Shiki tried to change this. He suggested that slang and even Western words could be used in haiku. He felt that the poet should be allowed to express nature and human life as he or she sees it, without sticking to rules and formulas. He suggested that it was fine to write a haiku about winter in summertime, since the haiku was now separated from the *renga* and did not need dating. It was Shiki who first commonly used the word ''haiku'' for the small poems that had developed from *hokku*. Here is one of Shiki's haiku that reminds you haiku are just about seeing and not about judging whether a thing is beautiful or not:

*By a winter river
forsaken, a dog's
carcass!*

Fuyu-gawa   ni   /   sutetaru inu-no   /   kabane kana
winter-river at   /   forsaken dog's   /   remains !

Haiku:

Haiku Today

Not everyone agreed with Shiki, and today many Japanese still write traditional haiku within the 5-7-5 syllable framework, being sure to use a seasonal word, and allowing pauses by using "cutting" words. However, nowadays, with air conditioning and central heating and with most Japanese living in cities, seasonal words are more likely to be "Xmas sales" than "icicles." While people still do write haiku in the traditional style, you will find that many modern Japanese haiku are about Japan's industrial world, sometimes they do not include a seasonal word, and many vary from the 5-7-5 *onji* that are traditionally required.

Haiku are enormously popular in Japan, even today. All over Japan there are hundreds of clubs for haiku writers, many magazines just for the publication of haiku, and even newspaper haiku columns. One present haiku school (that is, a group of haiku writers who follow a master haiku poet) has 2,000 members and meets at a Zen temple or a place famous for its scenery in order to write haiku. Someone estimated that Japan has at least one million people who write haiku regularly.

If the history of haiku interests you, you will probably want to read more about it. For the moment, however,

tanka-renga-haikai-hokku-haiku

sums it up pretty neatly.

Before finishing our look at haiku, we should look at four areas that are associated closely with haiku. The first are journals that include haiku (*haibun*). The second are drawings that often accompanied the haiku (*haiga*). Third, we will look at haiku that make you laugh (*senryū*). And last, we will take a brief look at a women haiku writer.

Haibun – Haiku Diaries

Earlier I mentioned that Bashō enjoyed going on trips. He would be accompanied by close friends and students. Usually he would keep a travel diary and scattered throughout the diary would be haiku. You might like to read *Narrow Road to the Interior*, which was the most famous of Bashō's travel diaries. This mixture of prose and haiku was called *haibun*.

Issa also wrote *haibun* and his *My Spring* is very touching. In writing *haibun*, there is little explanation of the haiku in the prose, but the mood is the same.

It might surprise you, but both Bashō and Issa corrected and edited their diaries when they got back home. Sometimes they even included descriptions of events that had occurred at a different time. What they were aiming for was a perfect presentation, not an accurate account of their trip. Bashō, particularly, tried to make it seem that he was just an impoverished Buddhist wanderer, whereas, in reality, he often stayed at rich patrons' homes and usually had someone to help him find food and shelter.

Try keeping a diary for a week and noting down anything that strikes you as interesting about the weather, plants or animals. These notes are the makings for haiku. If you keep a diary regularly, you could add haiku where you feel strongly about something. It will make diary-keeping that much more interesting.

Haiga – Haiku Pictures

With small, spontaneous poems went small spontaneous illustrations. Just as the haiku is a brief poem, so the *haiga*, or picture that often accompanied a haiku, was just a suggestion of the subject that it was illustrating and was meant to be drawn in "one breath," just the same length of time that it takes to recite the haiku. *Haiga* don't illustrate haiku but merely suggest the scene. *Haiga* accentuate aspects of a subject that most people overlook. You rarely see details in *haiga* and often the scenery is very sketchy. They were drawn almost roughly and awkwardly. Sometimes the picture was painted first and then the haiku was added afterwards.

Buson was a great *haiga* painter and not only did he illustrate some of his own haiku, but as we mentioned earlier, he also added his pictures to Bashō's travel journals. *Haiga* were at their peak from the middle of the 17th century to the middle of the 19th century. These pictures were not of nobility but of simple things such as willow trees, sparrows, bamboo, cherry blossoms, gourds and crows. Professor Zolbrod, the noted authority on Noh drama and *haiga*, called haiku + *haiga*, "babble + doodle." If you draw a *haiga* when you are working on a haiku, it may help you picture the scene more clearly and help you with your choice of words.

Go back to the haiku you wrote while you were reading this book and add some "doodle" to them.

one breath poetry

Senryū – Witty Haiku

Often in the middle of *haikai no renga* there would be witty verses and these later developed into independent verses known as *senryū*. It is hard to tell the difference between a haiku and a *senryū*, but people seem to waste a lot of time trying to decide whether a verse is one or the other. You could say that *senryū* make you laugh at human foolishness, and haiku make you ponder or wonder. Traditional-style haiku usually have a seasonal word and a cutting word, unlike the *senryū*. *Senryū* are named after Karai Hachiemon (1718-1790), whose pen name was Senryū and who collected these witty lines of linked verse. In those days, the selectors were more famous than the poets who actually wrote the verse and so Senryū became very famous. It was said that he criticized over two and a half million poems in his lifetime. Here is a senryū by Yayu.

You foolish scarecrow
under your stick feet
birds are stealing the beans.

A very similar one was written by Maria Gumabon from Guam when she was in Grade 5:

Crows sit on his arms
he tries to scare them away
straw in ragged clothes.

Haiku:

THE HISTORY OF HAIKU

Here is a poem by 13-year-old Ashley of Canada (no surname given), which appeared in *Haiku by the Children*. If laughter is a sign, this verse might certainly qualify as a senryū:

Small green growing things
in my old dirty locker
on my ham sandwich.

It certainly has a "what" and "where," though you are left to wonder about the "when."

Brenden Jeffery of Australia wrote this amusing verse when he was nine:

The cyclone comes down
as we watch the late movie
darn the power's gone.

When you see something that makes you smile, try to write a senryū about it.

Women and Haiku

A haiku is a haiku whether it is written by a child or an adult, a male or a female. You may have noticed that most of the traditional writers of haiku in Japan were men. That was because women were not encouraged to be educated, particularly in learning the Chinese style of writing that was the script for early poems. Japanese women could, however, write in hiragana, a simplified form of the Chinese letters thought suitable for women's "lesser minds."

Funnily enough, some of the best and best-remembered writers in Japanese literature were women. Lady Murasaki wrote the world's first novel, *Genji Monogatari*, which still makes great reading even today. Sei Shonagon, a court lady, wrote very sharply about the goings-on at court. There were also some good women haiku poets. My favorite is Chiyo-ni. Chiyo-ni means "the nun Chiyo." Her real name was Kaga no Chiyo. She lived from 1703 to 1775. She was married at 19, but her husband died and so did a little son. Many Japanese say she didn't write "real" haiku because her poems lacked depth and didn't set you thinking. That seems to be the opinion of those who defined haiku rules and those were all men. See what you think.

Haiku:

My favorite haiku of hers is about her small son who died. In this haiku, she uses a memory of him chasing dragonflies with a net, a common image in Japan even today:

My dragon-fly hunter:
where has he wandered today
I wonder?

tombo-tsuri	/	*kyō wa*	*doko*	*made*	/	*itta*	*yara*
dragon-fly-catcher	/	today	where	as far as	/	gone	wonder

Going to her well one day, Chiyo-ni finds that the well-bucket had been overgrown with the vinelike plant, morning glory. Rather than disturb it, she goes to her neighbor to borrow water.

Finding morning glories
have captured my well-bucket
I borrow water.

asagao	*ni*	/	*tsurube*	*torarete*	/	*morai*	*mizu*
morning-glories	by	/	well-bucket	imprisoned	/	accept	water

one breath poetry   65

Haiku:

Last Thoughts

███

You have now read quite a bit about haiku – how they are written in Japan and how you can write them in English, where they came from and who the famous haiku poets were. The question may have struck you, "Why bother with haiku?" Here are some of the reasons why I like haiku and think it is important to know how to read and write them.

* Haiku are a direct and immediate response to surroundings, so writing them keeps me aware of the present and not lost in memories of the past or dreams of the future.

* When I read translations of Japanese haiku, I am drawn to learn more about Japanese culture and history, particularly other Japanese arts that were influenced by Zen Buddhism, such as the tea ceremony and ikebana.

* I particularly enjoy reading *haibun*, and they have made me curious to read earlier travel diaries, particularly those of the ladies at the Heian court in Kyoto long ago.

* Writing haiku has forced me to use my words more carefully and to express my ideas more clearly.

* The more I see life in terms of little poems, the more I see the unity in all things. This makes me feel very open to all living things and the way we are linked.

* Most important of all, writing haiku helps me to appreciate the small things in everyday life.

Next time you start to write a haiku you may not reach for a brush as Bashō would have. But, whether you pick up a pencil or pen, or turn the computer on, pause a moment and feel how you are connected with the long line of haiku poets. Then take a breath and write.

one breath poetry

68

Haiku:

Bibliography

Younger Readers

Birds, Frogs and Moonlight by Cassedy, Sylvia, and Kunihiro Suetake. Illus. by Vo-Dinh. Garden City, N.Y.: Doubleday, 1967.

Bug Haiku by Hackett, J. W. Illus. by Earl Thollander. Tokyo: Japan Pub. Inc., 1968.

A Few Flies and I (Haiku by Issa). Selected by Merrill, Jean, and Ronni Solbert. Trans. by R. H. Blyth and Nobuyuki Yuasa. Illus. by Ronni Solbert. New York: Random House, 1969.

Haiku by Lewis, Florence. Portland, Maine: Walch, 1977.

Haiku by the Children. A Japan Air Lines sponsored competition. Japan, 1991.

The Haiku Moment, by SPICE. Slide kit. Stanford, Calif.: Stanford University, SPICE, 1977.

In a Spring Garden. Edited by Lewis, Richard. Illus. by Ezra Jack Keats. New York: Pied Piper-Dial Press, 1989.

In the Eyes of the Cat. Selected and illus. by Demi. Trans. by Tze-si Huang. New York: Holt, 1992.

Out of the Mouths. Compiled by JAL. Vancouver: JAL, 1987.

Red Dragonfly on My Shoulder. Trans. by Cassedy, Sylvia, and Kunihiro Suetake. Illus. by Molly Bang. New York: Harper Collins, 1992.

Wind in the Long Grass. Edited by Higginson, William J. Illus. by Sandra Speidel. New York: Simon & Shuster, 1991.

Intermediate Readers

Haiku. Selected by Hughes, Mary Dawson. Kansas City: Hallmark, 1970.

Haiku in English by Henderson, Harold. Rutland, Vermont: Tuttle, 1967. 0-8048-0228-9

A Haiku Journey. Trans. by Britton, Dorothy. Tokyo: Kodansha, 1974.

Japanese Haiku by Beilenson, Peter. Mount Vernon, N.Y.: Peter Pauper Press, 1955.

Narrow Road to the Interior by Bashō, Matsuo. Trans. by Sam Hamill. Illus. by Stephen Adiss. Boston: Shambala, 1991.

The Year of My Life. A translation of Issa's *Oraga Haru.* Trans. by Yuasa, Nobuyuki. Berkeley: University of California Press, 1960, 1972. 0-520-02328-5

Adult

A Chime of Windbells. Trans. by Stewart, Harold. Rutland, Vermont: Tuttle, 1969. 0-8048-0092-8

The Haiku Handbook (How to Write, Share and Teach Haiku) by Higginson, William J. New York: McGraw Hill, 1985. 0-07-028786-4

Haiku in English by Henderson, Harold. Rutland, Vermont: Tuttle, 1967, 1992. 0-8048-0228-9

A Haiku Journey. Trans. by Britton, Dorothy. Tokyo: Kodansha, 1974.

Haiku Painting by Zolbrod, Leon. Tokyo: Kodansha, 1982. 0-87011-560-X

Haiku:

BIBLIOGRAPHY

A History of Haiku (in 4 vols.) by Blyth, R. H. Tokyo: Hokuseido, 1964.

An Introduction to Haiku by Henderson, Harold G.(Garden City, N.Y.: Doubleday, 1958.

Issa: Cup-of-Tea Poems. Translated by Lanoue, David G. Berkeley: Asia Humanities Press, 1979. 0-89581-874-4

The Master Haiku Poet Matsuo Bashō by Ueda, Makoto. Toronto: University of Toronto, 1970. 0-87011-553-7

Matsuo Bashō by Ueda, Makoto. New York: Twayne. Toronto: University of Toronto, 1970.

Modern Japanese Haiku. Compiled by Ueda, Makoto. Toronto: University of Toronto, 1976. 0-8020-2147-6

Narrow Road to the Interior by Matsuo, Bashō. Trans. by Sam Hamill. Illus. by Stephen Addiss. Boston: Shambala, 1991. 0-87773-644-8

On Love and Barley: Haiku of Bashō by Stryk, Lucien. Honolulu: University of Hawaii, 1985. 0-8248-1012-0

One Hundred Famous Haiku by Buchanan, Daniel C. Elmsford, N.Y.: Japan Publications, 1973. 0-87040-222-6

Paper Doors. Edited by Shikatani, Gerry, and David Aylward. Trans. by David Aylward. Toronto: Coach House Press, 1981. 0-88910-228-7

Index